© **GOING FORWARD IN LIFE**
BY SANDEEP RAVIDUTT SHARMA

Table of Contents

Introduction IV

Going Forward in Life.. 1

© **GOING FORWARD IN LIFE**
BY SANDEEP RAVIDUTT SHARMA

Introduction

This book provides you with a list of **100 motivational quotes and thoughts** about LIFE, written with the blessings, consciousness, grace, and energy of **Shiva-Shakti**. I'm sure if you keep reading, referring, sharing these thoughts and quotes about LIFE, you may derive inspiration and develop a positive outlook and good understanding of various perspectives and facts. The twist and turns in life never end. Keep going forward with a smile and never turn back unless someone needs your help to stay on the righteous path. Live each moment of your life journey now and enjoy it to the fullest.

"Going forward in life denotes your journey of constant improvement in your attitude and approach aiming to be the best."

I sincerely hope, you will find this book amazing, interesting, rejuvenating, unique and constant source of inspiration.

Thank You and Happy Reading.

© GOING FORWARD IN LIFE
BY SANDEEP RAVIDUTT SHARMA

© Copyright 2018 Sandeep Ravidutt Sharma - All rights reserved.

In no way is it legal to reproduce, duplicate, or transmit any part of this document in either electronic means or in printed format. Recording of this publication is strictly prohibited and any storage of this document is not allowed unless with written permission from the publisher. All rights reserved. The information provided herein is stated to be truthful and consistent, in that any liability, in terms of inattention or otherwise, by any usage or abuse of any policies, processes, or directions contained within is the solitary and utter responsibility of the recipient reader. Under no circumstances will any legal responsibility or blame be held against the author / publisher for any reparation, damages, or monetary loss due to the information herein, either directly or indirectly. The author own all copyrights.

Legal Notice:
This book is copyright protected. This is only for personal use. You cannot amend, distribute, sell, use, quote or paraphrase any part or the content within this book without the consent of the author or copyright owner. Legal action will be pursued if this is breached.

Disclaimer Notice:
Please note the information contained within this book is for motivational, educational and knowledge sharing purpose only. Every attempt has been made to provide the reader accurate, up to date and reliable complete information. No warranties of any kind are expressed or implied. Readers acknowledge that the author is not engaging in the rendering of legal, financial, medical or professional advice. By reading this document, the reader agrees that under no circumstances the author / publisher is responsible for any losses, direct or indirect, which are incurred as a result of the use of information contained within this document, including, but not limited to, —errors, omissions, or inaccuracies.

If you have further questions, contact on
Tel: +919969256731
Email: sandeepraviduttsharma@gmail.com

© GOING FORWARD IN LIFE
BY SANDEEP RAVIDUTT SHARMA

Dedication

This book is dedicated to **Goddess Bhairavi**. In the Hindu religion, the Goddess Bhairavi represents divine anger and wrath which is directed towards impurities within us as well as to the negative forces that obstructs our spiritual growth. Bhairavi Mata is also called as **Shubhamkari** and does good things. She is often depicted in images as holding a book, rosary and making abhaya and varada mudra with her hands. She is fiercely protective, lending us wisdom and power, steadiness and clarity. She personifies light and fire, supporting us to reveal what we keep hidden and inviting us to explore our hidden mind and any secret darkness.

I hereby recite the following Bhairavi mool mantra...
"Om Hreem Bhairavi Kalaum Hreem Svaha"
And pray to **Goddess Bhairavi** for lending wisdom and power, steadiness and clarity in the life of my readers and the world. May Goddess Bhairavi protect us from negative forces along with removing impurities of our mind.

GOING FORWARD
IN LIFE

© GOING FORWARD IN LIFE
BY SANDEEP RAVIDUTT SHARMA

Be the refreshing solution rather than the depressing problem.

People may find hundreds of ways to discourage and humiliate you. All you need to learn and implement is one single rule to remain Human and Humble.

© GOING FORWARD IN LIFE
BY SANDEEP RAVIDUTT SHARMA

You have little control over the flow of events except for your own actions.

© **GOING FORWARD IN LIFE**
BY SANDEEP RAVIDUTT SHARMA

Seek happiness on a full-time basis.

© GOING FORWARD IN LIFE
BY SANDEEP RAVIDUTT SHARMA

Time borns young every second.

Good things in life comes easy only when your intentions are good.

Weave the Flag of unity to wave at the fighting mob and make them one who have embraced peace ultimately.

If we sit and understand each others perspective, the solution is around the corner.

Be positive in your thoughts, approach and attitude.

Write your own story with ink of joy and words of happiness.

You can gift the entire world your humility and kindness. Return gift is assured in the form of smile and gratitude.

People like those who plan to share and not rule.

Let the churning of thoughts continue and produce innovation.

Beautiful moments are always there for you, all you need is a beautiful heart and vigilant mind to see the beauty around you. Remember...Life is beautiful so are you...

As you grow in life the challenges will multiply to test you further.

Get inspiration from the Moon. Alone it lights the world and fights darkness at a time when the sun has retired and Stars are playing hide n seek game.

You don't need to shout when the truth is on your side.

God made Man not to harass the other species but to protect them.

Silence is Golden. It's true only when it is practiced at the right time, mostly when you know that your words will not make much of an impact.

Go ahead with your plans if you intend to achieve your goals.

The canvas of life is bigger than the sea. You can draw whatever you want.

Time can fly without any wings. You can also fly by the power of your mind and can even go into the future and the past. But remember... Time has seen it all...while you are not aware whether you will burn your wings or add another set of wings to fly fast. The best thing to do is Live NOW.

You can live your dreams only when it ends into your deeds in the real world.

Give up your overthinking and learn to live with your positive thoughts.

At times flow of thoughts doesn't seem to end. Capture and present the positive ones, it may benefit someone for whom the thought originated in this Universe and selected you as the messenger.

The smile is the greatest gift of God to mankind. Spend it as much as possible. Hoarding will make you cry.

Assumptions of any kind can hamper our decision.

Your single win can wipe out your decades of failure. Go for it. You can do it.

If you are troubled by your thoughts, remember it's the creation of your own mind, and you can change it anytime. Thoughts can make or break you in seconds.

If you are looking for the road to success, no such road exists in this world. You are the one who has to create this road with your sheer determination and efforts.

Kind heart possesses love in abundance.

You can't build your house overnight, brick by brick the structure is built.

© **GOING FORWARD IN LIFE**
BY SANDEEP RAVIDUTT SHARMA

You may like the Blue Sky but that doesn't mean ... Sky stops showing the world it's many moods through different colours.

Sitting at one place without doing nothing helps at times when you have been running throughout.

The beautiful and handsome pair looks richer and amazing with a kind heart.

A strong mind doesn't wait for approval from others.

Giving excuses can be easy, but it cannot change your position of failure. So please, stop giving excuses instead give a commitment.

It's easy to laugh or criticise someone. But it is much easier to understand their perspective and get enlightened or become the torch bearer.

Begin and end your day with a smile.

The world would be so boring to live if there is no laughter. Befriend laughter.

At times even your shadow gets lost in the darkness. Keep the candle of positivity burning at any cost.

Believe in your own self to achieve your dreams.

People talk about your vision only when you have lived to make it a reality.

Simplicity doesn't cost much, it only requires the change of habits.

Hard work is fine but smart work can make you a winner.

The Rich wants to get richer, there is nothing wrong in that act. But with each Dollar added, the moral responsibility of the rich towards helping or supporting the downtrodden increases. The question is whether the rich takes this as their responsibility in the first place.

You can't buy success map as no one knows how to draw it accurately.

Hold the hand of HOPE and leave EXPECTATIONS.

The healthy relationship is one where you don't force your will over the other.

© GOING FORWARD IN LIFE
BY SANDEEP RAVIDUTT SHARMA

As you grow in life seriousness takes over and in most cases, you tend to forget the humour, laughter, innocence, and secret of happiness known to you in your childhood. Don't let the child in you die.

Those who wear a watch just for style may not mind the delay.

In the absence of a leader, the crowd only knows how to talk. Be the leader and not the crowd.

The day you stop worrying about what the world will think and say, you will enjoy complete freedom.

Stay young at your heart and not by age.

Don't just plan but execute.

Your enthusiasm and die-hard attitude make you feel liberated from all kinds of worries.

The purpose of your life appears before you the day realization dawns on you to find it.

Believe and say to your own self that I have given my best today. Tomorrow will be another day. I would improve upon my today's performance.

The giant wheel doesn't really look big when you are on top of it. It looks like a Giant when you watch it from the ground. The same principle applies to our life problems. Using your knowledge and positive attitude, you can decimate any problem and win.

Going downhill require control and uphill needs your energy and persistence. Be consistent and have self-belief whichever way you choose to go.

Be one with Nature... Nature presents a free bouquet of happiness. Do you appreciate or keep ignoring, as you are busy doing things except living your life?

Life of its own is not easy. We are the ones designated by the creator to make it easy.

If your a seller, fulfill your promise by delivering the best to your customer.

Don't let your past steal your today. Live in the present.

Don't read for the namesake if you don't intend to understand.

You cannot hide your true happiness. Let the happiness shine and encourage others to be happy.

Positive thoughts come uninvited to live in the house of the beautiful mind. Welcome them.

Time is running in the fast lane and leaving behind everything. Don't compete with time rather focus on making the optimum use of time to improve the wellness quotient.

God has chosen you for a specific purpose. Find your purpose in life.

Those who often play with the emotion of others are cruel and inhuman. Respect the emotions and be human in your approach.

Simplicity is the key to living a satisfied life. Solution to the most complicated situation is always simple.

Celebrate life not just today but every day of your existence.

Seems to be complex yet simple

You get to know new things in life as well as meet newer faces when you say, 'I am available.' People who claim to be busy always are likely to lose a lot.

The single act of kindness can transform into a million smiles.

Goals help you to move forward.

The brick walls can't limit your ideas to flow further if you want.

The stone has outlived Men who created history by remaining mute. Silence helps one to survive difficult times.

Thank God for each day and moment. Make the best out of it. Be happy.

Wind chimes draw your attention towards the sound of joy coming closer to you. Take out some time to rhyme with the chime and refresh your mind.

Arrogance breeds hatred while humility attracts humanity.

Celebrate your success but remember it brings with it immediate and long term responsibility.

There is nothing wrong in getting attracted to the distraction with the code name Love.

If the present blurs out and the future looks uncertain. Stay calm and positive spending time to enhance or acquire new skills. As time passes over, the clarity will soon emerge and gives you the opportunity to be the winner again.

Holding the grudge against others is a sure shot way of cultivating unhappiness. Forgive, and you become richer and happy every minute.

You don't have to be as tall as the hill but with good deeds, one can achieve the highest summit of life.

Helpless ones are those who can't even cry. Be ready to lift them and bring smile on their face.

The world may end today or tomorrow. How does it matter to the one who is living NOW?

Wishes are many but means to achieve them are limited. Instead of limiting your wish it's better to focus on finding newer means.

If you want to lead then don't let others tell you what to do. You need to figure out and do.

Those who hold enormous power have to act with more responsibility.

Happiness matters. Don't wait for happiness to come to you. Grab it at first sight.

Wave at opportunities to welcome if you see one.

At times the vision gets blurred due to darkness spread in your mind. Open the window of your mind and let positivity sneak into it; every visual would be Crystal clear.

Opportunity never tells you that it's about to vanish. Identify in time and make most out of the Opportunities available.

World cheers for the winner. If you are still a winner in the making, you are also part of the cheering crowd. Feel the cheer and visualise it for your win. Cheer and Gear.

© GOING FORWARD IN LIFE
BY SANDEEP RAVIDUTT SHARMA

One should remember that most of the things connected with our lives are temporary. Be it your near and dear ones, your friends, place, thoughts, and even yourself. You have changed over the years and appears in a different form each day. When one knows that almost everything connected to us is temporary, still we crave for them. Attachment to all such temporary things is quite natural. Learned people say that our soul is eternal. It is in sync with the supreme self also known as the creator. One who practices detachment is rare amongst us. Staying detached amidst temporary beings is something one should practice only when self-realisation is achieved so friends till then stay connected.

Understand the world by starting with self.

The positive attitude can lift you up even when everyone else is drowning.

Be part of the crowd when you are fighting for the common cause and not when you are competing to win the leader slot.

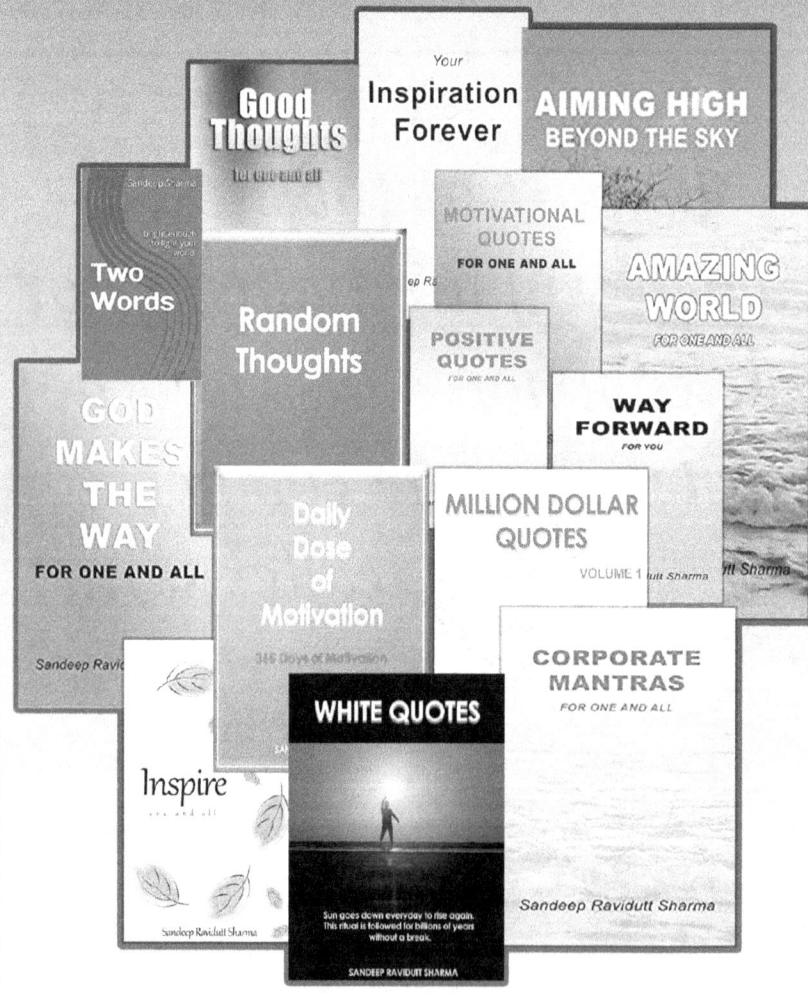

www.ingramcontent.com/pod-product-compliance
Lightning Source LLC
Chambersburg PA
CBHW070422220526
45466CB00004B/1506